ANC

A GUIDE TO AN
ON THE ISI

CW00542626

M. J. Yates BA, PhD, FSA and **David Longley** BA, FSA

Contents

Edited by Diane M. Williams BA, MA, PhD
Designed by Staziker Jones

First Published 1989, Second Edition 1994, Third Edition 2001

© *Cadw: Welsh Historic Monuments (Crown Copyright),*
Crown Building, Cathays Park, Cardiff, CF10 3NQ.

Printed in Great Britain by South Western Printers Ltd

ISBN 1 85760 142 4

Left: *A watercolour painting of Trefignath burial chamber. It was probably painted by the antiquarian scholar, William Owen Stanley (1802–84), about 1874 (Lord Stanley of Alderley).*

The island of Anglesey is justifiably renowned for its rich collection of ancient and historic sites which has long attracted antiquarians and archaeologists. The group of huts at the foot of Holyhead Mountain is one such site. Pioneering excavations were undertaken here by William Owen Stanley in the mid-nineteenth century and the site was further investigated between 1978 and 1982 revealing a period of extended occupation from at least 500 B.C. through to the post-Roman centuries. This view shows one of the excavated huts now laid out for public display (Mick Sharp Photography).

ARCHAEOLOGICAL AND HISTORICAL BACKGROUND

INTRODUCTION

The island of Anglesey has a personality all of its own. Sheltered in the lee of Snowdonia, it is the only area of fertile and accessible land in a region of high and barren mountains. It is, therefore, perhaps not surprising that settlers have been drawn to its shores from the dawn of history and beyond.

At the end of the twelfth century the scholar-cleric Gerald of Wales (d. 1223) quoted the already age-old name for the island, '*Môn mam Cymru*' — *Mona* the mother of Wales. He also recorded that 'when crops failed in all other regions, this island, from the richness of its soil and its abundant produce, has been able to supply all Wales'. Even allowing for a journalistic turn of phrase, Gerald's observation highlights the agricultural importance of Anglesey, which has continued through the centuries down to today.

Although it is Anglesey's fertility that sets it apart from the mountains of the mainland, the sea has also played an important role in shaping the island's historical fortune. Separated from the rest of Wales by the Menai Strait, Anglesey enjoyed easy contact with more distant regions across the Irish Sea. This is reflected in the early settlement of the island and in the many field monuments that punctuate the landscape today.

Indeed, it is this rich source of ancient and historic monuments that has long attracted antiquarians and archaeologists to Anglesey. They bear witness to the importance of the island and provide an exceptional opportunity to trace its history from early prehistoric times through to the medieval centuries. From the early enquiries of the Reverend Henry Rowlands (1655–1723) at the end of the seventeenth century and the pioneering excavations of Lord Stanley (1802–84) in the mid-nineteenth century, archaeological study has advanced and more recent excavations and historical research have revealed a complex pattern of human settlement, conflict and achievement on this island.

In the following pages you will find a brief introduction to the archaeology and history of Anglesey. This provides a broad chronological context for the twenty-three field monuments on the island that are in the care of Cadw: Welsh Historic Monuments. The site descriptions have been arranged into three 'tours' (see back cover) and each itinerary should make a comfortable day's outing, though the monuments can be visited easily in different sequences. The map on the inside back cover shows the period to which each monument belongs, and should enable visitors who are interested in a specific period to identify those sites they may particularly wish to visit.

Many of the monuments are small in comparison to some of the spectacular medieval castles for which Wales is so well known. They are sometimes difficult to get to, reached only by crossing agricultural land or uneven terrain, but this should not deter you. In return for a little effort, you will discover fascinating insights into the ways of life, the beliefs and the customs of many generations of the island's inhabitants.

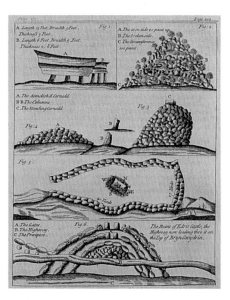

A page from Henry Rowlands's Mona Antiqua Restaurata.

Today, the only remains of Mesolithic occupation on Anglesey are scattered finds of the stone tools used by hunter-gatherer communities. This imaginative reconstruction shows how people may have lived around 7000 B.C. The rich natural resources of the island were doubtless attractive, with such communities selectively hunting game, fishing and collecting fruits. They may have occupied sites on a seasonal or short-term basis (National Museum of Wales).

THE MESOLITHIC: THE FIRST SETTLERS
(ABOUT 8000–4000 B.C.)

About 10,000 years ago, when the glaciers of the last Ice Age had finally retreated northwards across Britain, the climate improved dramatically with temperatures rising to almost present day levels. The rapid transition from cold tundra-like conditions was marked by the spread of trees, first birch and pine, then hazel. As temperatures continued to rise, woodland became more extensive until by about 6000 B.C. broad-leaved, deciduous trees, such as oak and elm, covered all but the rockiest and wettest parts of the island.

The first settlers on Anglesey may have arrived some time around 8000 B.C. They left few traces, but the discovery of their tools, particularly those made of imperishable materials such as flint and stone, has suggested they were nomadic people who relied for their food on animals they could hunt in the forests and fish caught in the sea. No doubt they also ate wild fruits and nuts, as well as shellfish and other food that could be gathered on a seasonal basis. They have left no evidence of permanent structures, but flint tools found beneath a later Bronze Age burial mound at Trwyn Ddu, near Aberffraw, and beneath the Iron Age hut circles at Holyhead Mountain (p. 43) suggest that some camps may have been occupied for extended periods.

THE EARLIER NEOLITHIC: THE FIRST FARMING COMMUNITIES
(ABOUT 4000–3000 B.C.)

By around 4000 B.C. techniques of farming, which had developed in the Near East, were gradually being adopted in Britain alongside existing hunting and gathering practices. New species of cultivated wheat and barley were grown and domesticated animals, including sheep and goats, were introduced. Crops required light and animals needed pasture, so the natural forest had to be cleared for both. Initially, small clearings provided space and it is possible that the earliest farmers moved from one area to another as soil fertility was exhausted.

Increasingly, communities no longer had to travel great distances in search of food and they could plan production to ease the effects of seasonal change. Manipulation of the environment intensified and — perhaps for the first time — people were able to establish a bond with a particular territory which they could settle and farm.

The evidence for domestic buildings is tantalizingly scarce; most were of timber, which has long since decayed. Occasionally, however, postholes have been found, such as those at Llandegai, near Bangor, where the outline of a large single building has been identified.

Pottery, too fragile for a nomadic lifestyle, came into use at this time and does sometimes survive, together with stone tools, to indicate domestic activity. Discovery of such evidence is often accidental — for example beneath later burial monuments such as Trefignath (p. 46). However, further study of the places where flint and stone tools have been found may help to identify more tangible evidence of settlement.

The most familiar Neolithic implement is perhaps the stone axe, which was used not only to clear the forest, but also to make utensils, and shape timber for building. Such axes appear to have been favoured items for they are often found far from the source of the stone from which they are made (see box feature below).

In contrast to the scant evidence for Neolithic settlement, it is the ritual and funerary monuments of the period that have left a durable mark on the landscape. Most notable are the so-called megalithic tombs, though recent debate amongst archaeologists has led to the suggestion that these 'tombs' had a much more complex role in society than simply as graves for the dead. The styles of tomb vary, but most comprise one or more burial chambers built of large stones set on end, usually covered by massive capstones that formed a roof. Although it is the huge stones that attract attention today, the chambers are likely to have been covered by a mound of earth or a cairn of stones. This would have focused attention on the entrance, which was sometimes marked by a forecourt area or imposing portal stones, as at Din Dryfol (p. 36).

Megalithic tombs have been studied extensively and many have been excavated. Nevertheless the majority of those on Anglesey do

---

NEOLITHIC STONE AXES

Two Neolithic stone axes made of volcanic rock from Graig Lwyd, Penmaenmawr. Graig Lwyd was an important source for stone axes. 'Rough-outs' would have been shaped at the 'axe factory' itself prior to transport to a lowland site for polishing. Analysis of stone axes found over a wide area has revealed that products from Graig Lwyd were used on a large scale and travelled far from their source, particularly to areas where there was no suitable stone for production. The axe on the left is a 'rough-out' from Graig Lwyd, and that on the right is a polished example found at Rhosybol on Anglesey (National Museum of Wales).

The gradual adoption of farming during the earlier Neolithic may have prompted a more settled way of life, and this in turn could have led to more permanent settlements. This imaginative reconstruction shows a Neolithic farming community of around 4000 B.C. (National Museum of Wales).

not fall readily into the classifications identified elsewhere and remain somewhat enigmatic.

Clearly they were intended to receive human remains and the identification of up to thirty individuals within the chamber at Lligwy (p. 28) suggests that at least one of their functions was to serve as burial vaults. The tombs often remained open to receive burials over many years, sometimes with earlier deposits moved to make way for additional bodies. Construction was sometimes complex, and excavation at Trefignath has shown how the form of a tomb could develop over several centuries, perhaps as ideas, associations and memories changed.

It is debatable whether such monuments served the entire community or were reserved for select families, or other sections of society. But the collection of massive stones and the raising of capstones weighing many tons would have required organized labour and probably represent significant communal effort. The tombs may also have served as a focal point for other ceremonies: at the entrance to some burial chambers excavation has revealed evidence suggestive of ritual activity. Although the nature of such ceremonies is elusive, it is not

impossible to imagine the importance which early agriculturists must have attached to their land, and the significance of ancestral burial in reaffirming their rights and beliefs. Such prominent structures could have represented stability and continuity within a now more permanently settled landscape.

THE LATER NEOLITHIC: AN AGE OF MONUMENTS
(ABOUT 3000–2500 B.C.)

As the Neolithic progressed, grander and more complex structures were built. Large, roughly circular enclosures defined by an earthen bank with an internal ditch are characteristic of the period. Known as 'henges', these monuments are not common in Wales, though a small example existed at Bryn Celli Ddu before the construction of the later tomb (p. 31) and two examples have been excavated at Llandegai, near Bangor. The function of these enclosures remains uncertain, but they can perhaps be seen as ceremonial centres serving communities drawn from a wide area.

A henge-like structure, dated to the Neolithic, was also built at Castell Bryn Gwyn (p. 34), but here the ditch lay outside the bank and excavation suggested a more prosaic function as a defended settlement. Although such settlements are rare, they have been recognized elsewhere in Britain.

Tombs also became more elaborate at this time and Anglesey has two very fine examples. At Bryn Celli Ddu it seems that the earlier henge — together with the circle of stones set within its ditch — was intentionally built over with a new style of monument known as a passage grave. These tombs, characterized by a long passage leading to a burial chamber, are found predominantly around the Irish Sea area; their presence on Anglesey serves to emphasize the opportunities provided by the sea to link the island with an extensive seaboard area. The connection is further emphasized by another passage grave, at Barclodiad y Gawres (p. 36), where the chambers are built of stones decorated with abstract spirals and zig-zags similar to those found on the passage graves of Ireland and Brittany.

Above: *Stones decorated with incised patterns of spirals and zig-zags have been found at various burial chambers along the western seaboards of Britain and Europe. This example is from Newgrange in the Boyne valley, Ireland.*

Right: *An illustration of one of the decorated stones inside Barclodiad y Gawres.*

The later Neolithic burial chamber of Barclodiad y Gawres belongs to a group of tombs known as passage graves — probably the latest type to emerge on Anglesey. Inside, several stones are decorated with spirals and zig-zags.

The pair of impressive standing stones at Penrhos Feilw on Holy Island, which perhaps date from the Bronze Age when such monuments seem to have become more common.

THE EARLIER BRONZE AGE: MONUMENTS AND METAL
(ABOUT 2500–1500 B.C.)

The discovery of copper and the development of bronze (an alloy of tin and copper) represented major technological advances, which enabled the manufacture of a new range of more effective tools and weapons. There is evidence that copper ore was mined in north Wales from the beginning of the Bronze Age and it is probable that the extensive reserves at Parys Mountain were being exploited from this time.

At the same time we see changes in burial traditions. Single graves replace communal vaults and instead of tombs being left open for additional bodies or bones, each burial was closed, perhaps reflecting greater emphasis on the individual. Cremation became increasingly common and so too did the practice of depositing items with the dead. To begin with pottery vessels, especially the distinctive 'beaker' style, accompanied inhumation burials, but gradually urns — often highly ornamented with impressed decoration — were used to hold cremated remains.

Tools, weapons and items of personal decoration sometimes accompanied burials. Beads of bone and knives of flint (still widely used in the Bronze Age) have been found with early Bronze Age burials on Anglesey, but occasionally more precious objects have also been recovered. Buttons and beads of jet, amber, and faience (a blue glass made in the eastern Mediterranean) demonstrate contact and trade with communities many miles away, and perhaps reflect the status of the person buried.

Tools and weapons of bronze have also been found with some burials. Given the work required to mine the ore, smelt the metals, prepare the bronze and cast the final object, these items must have been very highly prized. Deposition with a burial might again suggest an individual of both wealth and power.

Compared with the Neolithic, and indeed with Bronze Age monuments elsewhere, the funerary monuments of this period on Anglesey are not spectacular. Burials were often covered by round mounds or 'barrows' and originally these would have been impressive landscape features. Excavation has revealed complex funerary architecture with kerbs and stone

The distinctive form of pottery known as 'beaker' ware appeared on Anglesey in the earlier Bronze Age, as it did elsewhere in Britain. This vessel, from a single inhumation burial in the Merddyn Gwyn barrow at Pentraeth, is decorated with a herringbone pattern of incised chevrons. A bronze dagger and jet pin were also recovered from the grave (National Museum of Wales).

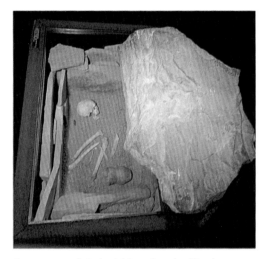

A reconstructed cist burial from Brymbo, Wrexham, showing the skeleton of a man buried with a beaker and flint knife. The change from communal to individual burial was accompanied by the appearance of elaborate grave goods (National Museum of Wales).

A cape of beaten gold from Mold, Flintshire, which accompanied an individual burial. It is perhaps one of the most ostentatious prehistoric grave goods to be found in the British Isles (British Museum).

Stonehenge, in Wiltshire, is perhaps the most famous and evocative prehistoric site in Britain. Its constructional history spanned some two millennia, between about 3100 and 1100 B.C., and in its final form appears to demonstrate a concern with the forces of nature (English Heritage).

A section of the rubble-built stone rampart enclosing the hillfort of Caer y Tŵr on Holyhead Mountain. Defended hilltop enclosures are known to have made their first appearance in the later Bronze Age, but a renewed and more extensive phase of construction began in the Iron Age.

features but now most have been levelled and there is little to see.

Other ceremonial monuments continued to feature in the landscape and perhaps owe something to Neolithic practices. The stone circle that lay within the henge at Bryn Celli Ddu has already been noted (pp. 6–7), and the same tradition can perhaps be seen in the standing stones — such as the pair at Penrhos Feilw (p. 46) — which are such a feature of the island. Their function, like that of the stone circles, is uncertain, but alignment with astronomic features suggests they could have played a part in the prediction and celebration of astral events.

THE LATER BRONZE AGE AND THE IRON AGE: FORTS AND FARMS
(ABOUT 1500 B.C.–A.D. 60)

From the middle of the second millennium B.C. evidence for ritual and funerary monuments becomes scarce, and for the first time the remains of widespread settlement can be identified. By the end of this period, around A.D. 60, centuries of woodland clearance had opened extensive tracts of countryside. Agriculture thrived and it is probable that much of the landscape was now managed for production, with extensive field systems surrounding established farming settlements.

On Anglesey, stone in preference to timber (now presumably in poor supply) was used for domestic building and an exceptionally fine example of Iron Age settlement can be seen in the hut circles on Holyhead Mountain (p. 43). Although not all the huts need have been inhabited at the same time this site does provide an insight into the density of settlement. In contrast, the settlement at Din Lligwy (p. 30) is distinguished by unusually large circular hut foundations with rectangular structures all within a large polygonal enclosure. The layout visible today probably dates from Roman times, but parallels elsewhere in north-west Wales suggest that the settlement may have originated in the Iron Age.

An increasing population and a deteriorating climate imposed new pressures on the landscape and encouraged greater competition for resources. It appears that people were forced to pay greater attention to their own

The increase in the appearance of weapons such as these swords in the later Bronze Age may indicate the growth of a more overtly aggressive society (National Museum of Wales).

protection and this seems to be reflected in the archaeological record. Swords, rapiers, and daggers become widespread in the later Bronze Age, to be replaced gradually by stronger iron weapons from the sixth century B.C.

Throughout prehistory the threat from natural predators and competitors such as wolves and wild boar meant settlements of all periods were often enclosed in some way. During the first millennium B.C., however, enclosures become more impressive and take on the appearance of serious fortifications. Comparison with the Iron Age defended settlement at Bryn Eryr, Llansadwrn, suggests that the enclosure at Caer Lêb (p. 34) may also date from this time. Here, the settlement was protected by two substantial earthen banks and a large ditch.

Other settlements took advantage of strong naturally defended positions, which were further protected by massive ramparts of earth, timber or stone. Caer y Twr (p. 44), on the summit of Holyhead Mountain, is an excellent example of such a hillfort, surrounded by a strong stone wall and protected on two sides by a steep natural drop. Unfortunately, there is no evidence of the houses of the inhabitants and it has been argued that such strong fortifications were only used in times of trouble rather than for everyday life.

Although agriculture underpinned the Iron Age economy, the number of hillforts throughout Britain suggests a preoccupation with defence and warfare. Often the ramparts were complex and occasionally excessive, suggesting that the

THE LLYN CERRIG BACH HOARD

Although funerary monuments are rare, we know from Roman writers that ritual played an important part in Iron Age culture. Alas, little tangible evidence has survived, but the discovery of valuable goods, sometimes intentionally damaged and deposited in wetland or at the water's edge, suggests votive offerings, perhaps to water spirits.

One of the best known examples comes from Llyn Cerrig Bach, near Valley on Anglesey. Here decorative bronze work, horse harness, and a selection of iron tools and weapons were discovered together with two carefully crafted iron gang-chains intended to secure human captives or slaves by the neck. These items provide an insight into the darker side of Iron Age culture where slavery and sacrifice played their part.

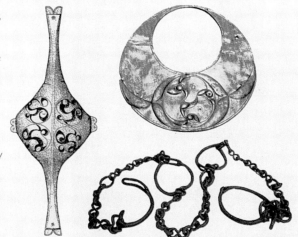

Left: *A shield boss with rich decoration found in the hoard.*
Top: *The ornately embossed bronze plaque from the hoard.*
Bottom: *One of the two iron gang chains from the Llyn Cerrig Bach hoard. It could have been used to manacle together four slaves or prisoners. (National Museum of Wales).*

The Chief Druid, as depicted in Henry Rowlands's Mona Antiqua Restaurata.

fortifications were intended as much to impress rivals as to keep them at bay. The scale of many hillforts presupposes a substantial labour force and sophisticated social organization managed by powerful tribal leaders.

THE ROMAN PERIOD: CONQUEST AND COEXISTENCE
(ABOUT A.D. 60–400)

Anglesey — or *Mona* — enters the light of history in the most dramatic way. In A.D. 43, 40,000 legionary soldiers and auxiliary troops of the Roman Emperor Claudius crossed the channel from Gaul and began the military conquest of southern Britain. By the year A.D. 60 the governor, Suetonius Paulinus, had reached the banks of the Menai Strait. He was not unopposed, as the Roman author, Tacitus, later records:

'Ranks of warriors lined the Anglesey shore, urged on by their women, shrieking like furies, dressed in burial black, while Druids, with arms outstretched to heaven, cursed the invaders.'
Tacitus, *Annals*, xiv, 30

THE DRUIDS

There are no surviving stone circles on Anglesey, though one possible site recorded in 1871 lay at Tre'r Dryw Bach, near Brynsiencyn. This same site may have been the one shown here in Henry Rowlands's Mona Antiqua Restaurata.

'It is thought that the Druidic system was invented in Britain and then imported into Gaul. It is to Britain that those wishing to make a more detailed study of it generally go to learn.' Julius Caesar

The status of the Druids was considerable. They seem to have been priests and men of learning, but they were also statesmen who advised kings and could arbitrate in regional disputes. They were theologians with a hint of the shaman and the guardians of ritual. Moreover, they presided over sacrifices from which the future was divined, and sometimes the sacrifices were human.

Following the invasion of Anglesey, Suetonius' troops cut down the *'sacred groves of the people, wherein lay their altars, red with the blood of sacrifice'*. Such vivid images encouraged antiquarian scholars, such as Henry Rowlands, to speculate on possible Druidic associations with Anglesey monuments of much greater antiquity.

The ensuing battle, which must have been a famously remembered Roman victory, is the only documented conflict between the Roman army and the enigmatic Druids (see box feature). Although the battle on the Menai was won, the victory was short lived. The revolt of Boudicca in the same year drew Suetonius back south and the conquest of the island was not consolidated until the late 70s, in the governorship of Agricola. Although the evidence is tenuous, a fort may have been garrisoned at Aberffraw under Suetonius. However, the nerve centre of Roman control and tax collection in north-west Wales for three centuries was to be the fort at *Segontium* (Caernarfon), which could have accommodated up to 1,000 auxiliary soldiers in the early decades after the conquest.

After the trauma of conquest, the communities in the countryside of Anglesey appear to have settled down to life under the new administration. Small farms seem to have prospered, many on sites that may have been in use during the Iron Age. However, the defences of coastal and hilltop fortifications are unlikely to have been maintained and there is something of an air of slightly dilapidated grandeur hanging over the settlements of middle-ranking noblemen. This is the pattern at the long-occupied and formerly defended Iron Age settlement at Bryn Eryr, Llansadwrn, which continued to be farmed during the Roman period. The history of Caer Lêb (p. 34) may have been similar.

A typical small farm comprised a few circular houses and, perhaps, additional rectangular structures, within a curvilinear or polygonal enclosure up to a quarter of an acre in extent. Where the evidence survives, walls are of stone, although the superstructure of the houses would have been of timber and thatch. Din Lligwy is a very fine example of such a farm (p. 30). Villages were rare although clusters of houses are known, such as those at Tŷ Mawr, Holyhead (p. 43). This settlement was certainly occupied during the Roman period.

Mixed farming was the economic mainstay of the countryside. Corn processing is indicated by the presence of simple saddle querns and mortars, as well as novel two-piece rotary querns. Cattle rearing must have been important, too. Although the evidence from settlements is scarce, the garrison at *Segontium* was well supplied with beef, which was almost certainly bought or levied from the

A Roman auxiliary infantryman of the second century. Up to 1,000 auxiliary soldiers could have been accommodated in the Roman fort at Segontium (Illustration by Geraint Derbyshire).

For three centuries the fort at Segontium was the centre of Roman control in north-west Wales (Skyscan Balloon Photography for Cadw: Welsh Historic Monuments).

The most characteristic form of native settlement in north-west Wales during the Roman period was the stone-built single farm or homestead, often associated with terraced fields. This artist's reconstruction is based on an excavated example at Cefn Graeanog on the Lleyn Peninsula. The settlements at Din Lligwy and Holyhead Mountain on Anglesey were probably of a similar nature (Illustration by Ivan Lapper, Reader's Digest).

The enclosed settlement of stone-walled round houses and rectangular buildings at Din Lligwy is a very fine example of a typical Anglesey farm of the Roman period (Gwynedd Archaeological Trust).

local countryside, including the pastures of Anglesey.

The trappings of Romanization reached the Anglesey countryside. These included commercially produced earthenware pots, small dress fittings in bronze, the occasional glass vessel and coins. The quantities were never great but they are sufficient to indicate contact with the Romanized market at the *vicus*, or settlement, which had grown up around the Roman fort at *Segontium*.

Most of the pottery in use on local farms was strictly utilitarian comprising cooking pots and jars. Occasionally an *amphora* has been found. These vessels once brought Gallic wine or Spanish olive oil to the port at *Segontium*. How far these sophisticated Mediterranean tastes permeated the countryside is not known, for discarded empty *amphorae* could have been reused as storage vessels. However, a number of families did possess a *mortarium*. These grit-studded bowls were used to grind and mash food and may be an indication of the adoption of certain Roman culinary habits. Some high quality tablewares were also in use — including prestigious Gaulish 'samian' glossy red ware — which must be seen as an adjunct to the status of their owners.

The presence of Rome was felt in other ways, too. Copper appears to have been mined at Parys Mountain in north-eastern Anglesey as early as the earlier Bronze Age (p. 9) and it seems that the ore resources were now exploited under Roman control. A series of stamped copper ingots from Anglesey does indeed suggest the significance of the Parys Mountain mines; so too does the discovery of a large courtyard house at *Segontium,* thought to be the residence of a senior official of procuratorial rank, stationed there to administer mineral exploitation along the north Wales coast.

During the later fourth century the Roman province of Britain was subject to incursions from both land and sea from a number of directions. Piracy was not an altogether new problem; from the late third century the channel coast had been fortified and garrisoned against pirates from beyond the mouths of the Rhine. Now, watchtowers were built along the Yorkshire coast, looking out over the North Sea against the possibility of longshore piracy from beyond the northern frontier. On the west coast, however, the threat appears to have come from the Scotti – the seaborne Irish. In response to this threat, Holy Island was provided with two new military installations that were designed to work in tandem. On the summit of Holyhead Mountain (Mynydd Tŵr), the highest point on the whole of Anglesey, a rectangular watchtower and signal station was built (p. 45). This lookout commanded extensive views across the Irish Sea. On the coast to the east, at the cliff-edge that marks the old shoreline overlooking Holyhead harbour, a small rectangular fort was constructed (pp. 42–3). The herringbone masonry walls, which now enclose St Cybi's church, are all that remain of this important outpost from where scouts and fast interceptor boats could be launched using the protected beaching on the shingle below.

To what degree this strategy was successful is not known. Later tradition remembers the settlement of north Wales by the Irish, while folk etymology understood the old stone-walled hut circle settlements of a forgotten past to be Irishmen's huts – *Cytiau'r Gwyddelod.* It is more likely, however, that the progressive removal of regular troops to fight more pressing continental engagements and a central government's pre-occupation with issues closer to the imperial core were responsible for the severing of links with the westernmost province of the Empire.

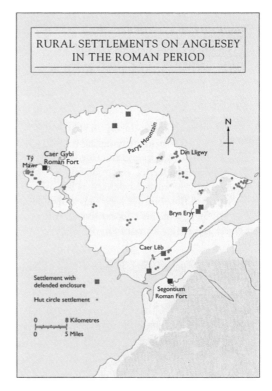

RURAL SETTLEMENTS ON ANGLESEY IN THE ROMAN PERIOD

Caer Gybi
Roman Fort
Tŷ Mawr
Parys Mountain
Din Lligwy
Bryn Eryr
Caer Lêb
Segontium
Roman Fort

Settlement with defended enclosure

Hut circle settlement

0   8 Kilometres
0   5 Miles

N

Above: *Copper has been mined at Parys Mountain since the Roman period and perhaps from as early as the earlier Bronze Age (David Longley, Gwynedd Archaeological Trust) .*

Inset: *A stamped copper ingot from the Roman mines at Parys Mountain (National Museum of Wales).*

THE EARLY MIDDLE AGES: THE AGE OF KINGSHIP
(ABOUT A.D. 400–1100)

'Britain has kings, but they are tyrants ... she has priests – but they are shameless, grabbers', wrote the cleric, Gildas, during the first half of the sixth century. By identifying the two key institutions of kingship and the Christian church he not only characterized the political framework of the early Middle Ages but also demonstrated the contrast with that which had gone before. It is in this context that Gwynedd emerged as a major kingdom in north-west

The walls of the late Roman coastal fort at Caer Gybi can be seen enclosing St Cybi's church. Although later, the church lies on the site reputedly granted to Saint Cybi, where a monastery developed that bears his name (Gwynedd Archaeological Trust).

A cast of the memorial in Llangadwaladr church to Cadfan, king of Gwynedd, who died about 625. The inscription indicates the survival of the use of Latin at this time (David Longley, Gwynedd Archaeological Trust).

Wales, early in the sixth century, if not before. A persistent tradition, recorded in the ninth century, remembered the arrival of a certain Cunedda and his sons, from the eastern lowlands of Scotland, as instrumental in the process. A dynasty was established and Irish settlers were expelled in an act of bloody ethnic cleansing. It is impossible now, however, to distil historical fact from legend. Nevertheless, a century later Cunedda's descendant, Maelgwn (d. about 547) — the 'Island Dragon' — was firmly in control. Later tradition, perpetuated in bardic rigmarole, identified Aberffraw on Anglesey, as one of the three tribal thrones of the island of Britain. And so, from early times, it may have been.

This was also an age when charismatic churchmen established a parallel power base alongside, and often with the support of, secular authority. Bangor Fawr — Great Bangor, Deiniol's monastery — was established on the mainland of Arfon during the sixth century. On Anglesey itself monastic foundations traditionally associated with St Seiriol and his contemporary, St Cybi, may be equally early. Tradition ascribes the foundation of Penmon to Seiriol in the sixth century, and a well associated with the saint can be seen at the site today (p. 24). Remains on nearby Puffin Island (Ynys Seiriol or Priestholm) have also been ascribed to St Seiriol. Caer Gybi is associated with St Cybi (p. 42). The area within the Roman walls of Caer Gybi is said to have been granted to Cybi, and here developed the monastery and later church, which bears his name.

Beyond these basic details, we know very little of the internal arrangements or the nature of the communities at these early monasteries, but we may be sure that the major establishments had the support and patronage of influential secular lords.

The seventh century was a time of ambition and conflict. Edwin of Northumbria and Cadwallon of Gwynedd clashed in a feud that eventually claimed both their lives. By the end of the century, however, Gwynedd, under the leadership of Cadwallon's son, Cadwaladr (d. 664), had recovered from the experience. The memorial to Cadwaladr's grandfather, Cadfan — 'the most wise and renowned of all kings' — in Llangadwaladr church perhaps highlights the extent of Gwynedd's ambition; it also suggests the presence of a royal chapel and burial ground close to the court of Aberffraw.

The royal centre at Aberffraw and the great churches on the island became the key targets for Viking raids. Penmon, located close to the shore, was attacked and ravaged in 971.

During the eighth and ninth centuries the kingdoms of Britain were subject to raids from the Vikings. Danish Vikings attacked the east coast in the 790s and by about 841–42, the Black Gentiles (Norwegians) had established an Irish Sea base at Dublin. In 855, *Brut y Tywysogyon* (*Chronicle of the Princes*) records that 'Anglesey was ravaged by the Black Gentiles'. Further raids are recorded during the ninth and tenth centuries when Holyhead, Aberffraw and Penmon were targeted. Around this time, a secular enclosed settlement at Glyn, near the coast at Red Wharf Bay, shows evidence first of conflict, followed by economic contact with the Viking world. Raids were tempered with trading; moreover, during the late eleventh and twelfth centuries the rulers of Gwynedd turned to Viking Dublin and the Isle of Man for refuge and military aid on numerous occasions.

This Irish Sea connection was always important. The second royal dynasty of Gwynedd — from which emerged the strong ninth-century kings Merfyn Frych (d. 844), Rhodri Mawr (the Great, d. 878) and Anarawd 'King of the Britons' — sprang from the marriage of Gwriad (who may have come from the Isle of Man) to Esyllt,

VIKING ARMLETS

These silver arm-rings of Viking character were found at a quarry on Red Wharf Bay, Anglesey. They were probably manufactured in Ireland, under Viking influence, where similar examples appear to have been used as a form of currency. The Anglesey find provides comparatively rare tangible evidence for the presence of the Norsemen on the island during the period of the invasions (National Museum of Wales).

COMMOTE, MAERDREF AND LLYS

The governance of medieval Gwynedd was peripatetic. The kings, and later the princes, supported themselves and their extensive retinues by travelling from region to region, drawing on the hospitality, food renders and work services provided by their clients and tenants. By the twelfth century the *commote* had become established as the manageable territorial unit for regional administration.

The prince maintained a royal estate, or *maerdref*, within each *commote* and it was here that he would stay on his royal circuit. Here were the royal halls and other important buildings. In the prince's absence the *llys*, or estate centre, would be maintained by royal officials who would also manage the tenants on the estate and supervise the food renders and work services from the *commote* generally.

During the twelfth and thirteenth centuries there were six *commotes* on Anglesey. The locations of five *maerdrefi*, with their *llysoedd*, are known. Very little, if anything, now survives to be seen above the surface of the ground, although at Rhosyr, Newborough, in the *commote* of Menai, excavations by the Gwynedd Archaeological Trust have revealed the foundations of a *llys*, its enclosure and internal buildings, which are now open to the public.

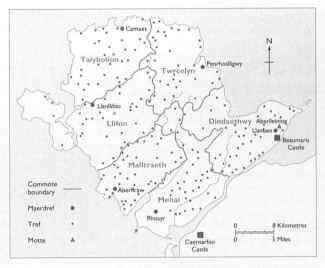

Anglesey under the princes, showing the division of the island into administrative regions, or commotes, and the location of the royal estates (maerdrefi) at the commotal centres. The map also shows the distribution of townships (trefi) and hamlets. There might be several homesteads in each community, ranging in size from the large home farms on the estates of freeholders to the smallholdings of bond tenants.

Reconstruction drawing of how the llys at Rhosyr may have looked in the mid-thirteenth century (Illustration by John Hodgson).

daughter of Cynan from Dindaethwy on Anglesey. The new succession of rulers accompanied, if not occasioned, a new vigour in the Gwynedd kingship. Its control expanded to include not only large areas of north Wales, but at times the rulers also held overlordship of the greater part of Wales. The career of Gruffudd ap Cynan (d. 1137) illustrates well the importance of the Irish Sea networks. Gruffudd, of the royal line of Anarawd and Rhodri, was born in exile in Ireland to the daughter of the Viking king of Dublin. In 1075 he began a long but ultimately successful battle to reclaim the kingdom of Gwynedd, often drawing on his Irish Sea connections. In the course of this struggle, he was to encounter an entirely new threat from the east — the Normans.

Following the conquest of England in 1066, the Norman king, William I (1066–87), encouraged powerful barons to establish great lordships along the borders of Wales and to encroach on Welsh territory. During the last two decades of the eleventh century, Norman control along the coast of north Wales extended into Gwynedd. In 1086 Robert of Rhuddlan (d. 1088) claimed to hold Gwynedd for King William (1066–87). By 1093 Hugh of Avranches (d. 1101), earl of Chester, was able to grant the rents from certain estates on Anglesey and fishing rights in the Menai Strait for the support of St Werbergh's Abbey in Chester, and a castle mound had been built at Aberlleiniog, near Penmon.

Gruffudd secured a notable victory in 1094 when he captured and burnt Aberlleiniog and other Norman strongholds, so 'delivering Gwynedd from castles'. In 1098, however, the Norman counter-attack threatened to reverse these gains entirely when, seemingly fortuitously, Magnus Barelegs' Viking fleet sailed into the Menai Strait. The ensuing battle destroyed the Norman grip on Gwynedd, allowing Gruffudd to take control of his destiny. One can only wonder what diplomatic exchange passed between Magnus and Gruffudd.

Having begun as a free-booting adventurer in the troubled waters along the Irish Sea coast, Gruffudd now emerged as a statesman who laid the foundations for the consolidation, growth and administrative reform that were to characterize the next 150 years — the age of princes.

The Norman Conquest was consolidated with the construction of earth-and-timber castles – as shown in this scene from the Bayeux Tapestry.

The castle mound at Aberlleiniog was built by Earl Hugh in the early 1090s, but was besieged and burnt by Gruffudd ap Cynan in 1094 (David Longley, Gwynedd Archaeological Trust).

THE AGE OF PRINCES AND THE LATER MIDDLE AGES
(ABOUT A.D. 1100–1600)

'*Every kind of good prevailed and Gwynedd then glittered with lime-washed churches, like the firmament with stars*'. Historia Gruffud vab Kenan.

The twelfth and thirteenth centuries were a period of expansion and administrative reform. In 1137, Gruffudd ap Cynan was succeeded by his son, Owain Gwynedd, who built successfully on his father's achievements. By his death in 1170 Owain had considerably extended the boundaries of Gwynedd. The earliest surviving stone churches on Anglesey date from this period and the island's prosperity can be assessed in the number of churches embellished in the Romanesque style and provided with decorated fonts — more than

Beaumaris Castle was begun in 1295 following the rebellion led by Madog ap Llywelyn. In order for the accompanying new town to flourish, nearby Llanfaes was depopulated and the community resettled at Newborough.

in any other region of north Wales. Penmon (p. 23) and the tower on Puffin Island (Ynys Seiriol or Priestholm) are fine examples. Hen Capel Lligwy (p. 29) also dates from this period.

During the thirteenth century two exceptional rulers — Llywelyn ab Iorwerth (the Great, d. 1240), and his grandson, Llywelyn ap Gruffudd (the Last, d. 1282) — for a time brought much of Wales under their control. In 1230, at the height of his power, Llywelyn the Great took for himself the unique title 'Prince of Aberffraw and Lord of Snowdon', emphasizing the link between the mountain stronghold of his kingdom and its spiritual and symbolic heart on Anglesey.

Before his death in 1240, Llywelyn the Great endowed one of the earliest Franciscan friaries in Wales as a memorial and burial place for his wife Joan, daughter of King John (1199–1216). It was also at about this time that the ancient monasteries at Bardsey, Beddgelert, Penmon and St Tudwal's Island adopted the Augustinian *Rule* and thereby accepted the framework of contemporary European monasticism. The Welsh princes encouraged these conversions, increasing endowments to support the new communities of Augustinian canons.

However, between 1276 and 1283 Gwynedd was drawn into two disastrous wars with the English king, Edward I (1272–1307). Llywelyn ap Gruffudd, lamented as 'the King, the oaken door, of Aberffraw', was killed on campaign near Builth in 1282, and with his death Gwynedd passed into the control of the English crown. The reorganization that followed saw the creation of the county of Anglesey. Resentment over injustices in the new administration eventually boiled over into revolt, and in 1294–95 the Welsh rose in rebellion led by Madog ap Llywelyn, a distant kinsman of the Gwynedd royal family.

In the aftermath of the revolt, Edward I began to build the last of his great castles in north Wales. The location, at Beaumaris, was well chosen to control the northern approaches to the Menai Strait from the Anglesey shore. Equally significant, the new site controlled an important ferry crossing from the mainland. The new town of Beaumaris, laid out with the castle, appropriated the flourishing sea-borne trade from nearby Llanfaes — whose Welsh community was now cynically resettled at

Newborough, in the west of the island. Nevertheless, both boroughs prospered: Beaumaris with its port and ferry and Newborough with its fairs and markets. And, for a while during the sixteenth century, Newborough replaced Beaumaris as the county town of Anglesey.

After the upheaval of war, bad weather and plague took their toll on the island during the earlier fourteenth century. The traditional tenurial pattern of land holding began to break down; nevertheless, those with an entrepreneurial flair prospered. The fine sculptures of Saints Pabo and Iestyn in their respective parish churches are monuments to the success and grateful generosity of one Anglesey landowner in the 1370s.

By the turn of the century Anglesey was at war again. In 1400 the island, described as 'the nursery of Welsh Nationalism,' became embroiled in the uprising led by Owain Glyn Dŵr. Henry IV (1399–1413) led a retaliatory attack on the friary at Llanfaes, where the Franciscans were sympathetic to Glyn Dŵr's cause, and inflicted serious damage. In 1403 the rebels laid siege to Beaumaris Castle, but by 1406, when records suggest that many living on the island had submitted to the king, the revolt in Anglesey seems to have been all but over.

But there was growth too. This was a time when large estates could be created, not through ties of kinship but, increasingly, through dealings in the property market. Fine examples of gentry houses of the fourteenth and fifteenth centuries survive at Hafoty, Llansadwrn and at Plas Berw.

The rise of the Tudor dynasty brought a greater degree of settled prosperity to the island. Henry VII (1485–1509) was a descendant of the Penmynydd branch of one of the most important and powerful dynastic families of Anglesey. This period gave rise to architectural developments that reflect contacts with England and, of course, the wealth generated by family connections at court. Important examples may be seen at the churches of Caer Gybi, Llaneilian and Beaumaris. Those at Caer Gybi and Llaneilian were among the oldest of Anglesey's religious foundations, and they continued to prosper as parish churches. But the sixteenth century also heralded a new age and with it the dissolution of equally ancient religious communities. Penmon was suppressed in 1536 and in 1539 Llanfaes passed into private hands to be dismantled, stone by stone.

The fine fourteenth-century memorial to St Pabo in Llanbabo church (Mick Sharp Photography).

The fourteenth-century hall-house at Hafoty, Llansadwrn, recently restored by Cadw: Welsh Historic Monuments.

St Seiriol's church and priory at Penmon, looking south-east across the Menai Strait. The existing church was probably begun around 1140–70, and was extended when it became an Augustinian priory in the first half of the thirteenth century.

THE ANGLESEY TOURS

In visiting all monuments, you should take care to keep to indicated pathways, and skirt the edges of ploughed fields. Stout footwear is advisable, especially at Caer y Tŵr (p. 44). An Ordnance Survey map (1:50,000 sheet no.114) is strongly recommended, and at some of the monuments a torch will help highlight the detail. Car-parking is not specifically available at all sites, and in some cases care is necessary when parking at the roadside.

TOUR 1
EASTERN ANGLESEY

Entering the island by the A55 across the Britannia Bridge, take the A4080 eastwards to Menai Bridge and continue on the A545 to Beaumaris. The original bridge was built by Robert Stephenson between 1846 and 1850, to carry the railway across the strait. A little to the east is Thomas Telford's suspension bridge of 1819–26.

You will probably wish to stop in Beaumaris and visit the magnificent castle. Begun for Edward I in 1295, it was the last and largest of the king's fortresses in north Wales. Here, his architect, Master James of St George, produced what is probably the most sophisticated example of medieval military architecture in the British Isles. A separate Cadw guidebook to the castle is available at the site.

On leaving the town, take the B5109 eastwards and follow the signs for Penmon and Penmon Point. As you enter Penmon, you will pass the deer park, established in the eighteenth century, possibly by the

sixth Lord Bulkeley. Beyond, to the north, is Puffin Island (Ynys Seiriol or Priestholm). On Puffin Island, the surviving church tower dates from the twelfth century, but it is thought to stand on the site of an earlier church. The island is privately owned, and is a 'Site of Special Scientific Interest'.

1–4 PENMON
Historical Background

(NGR SH630806)

There is a car park outside Penmon Priory.

The monuments to be seen at Penmon belong mainly to the post-Roman and later medieval periods. Traditionally, it is the site of a monastery established in the sixth century A.D. by St Seiriol, a friend and contemporary of St Cybi. The

Penmon Priory in 1742, drawn by Samuel and Nathaniel Buck. At the time, the building in the south-east corner of the cloister was still roofed.

holy well that survives may have its origins in this period. It seems likely that there was a monastery here throughout the seventh and eighth centuries, but there are no physical remains of early buildings standing above ground. Penmon was attacked during the Viking raids of the tenth century, and it is from about this time that the free-standing cross (no. 2) in the church belongs.

The present church was initially constructed about 1140–70, with the nave, central crossing and south transept dating to this period; and presumably it served the existing native Welsh monastic community. In the earlier thirteenth century, a new chancel, more than double the size of the existing nave, was added to the eastern end. Such a building programme is likely to have arisen when the community was reorganized as a body of Augustinian canons (p. 20).

Traditionally, the well and circular 'cell' at Penmon are associated with St Seiriol. The surviving remains, however, are very much later in date. The 'cell' may have been used by pilgrims in more recent times to prepare before bathing in the well waters (Mick Sharp Photography).

One of the two free-standing crosses from Penmon, which is now located in the south transept of the church. The head and shaft are carved from a single stone and decorated with intricate patterns.

A cloister was formed to the south (see plan, p. 26), which was fairly typical of medieval monastic planning, the southern range being occupied by the canons' dining hall. However, this arrangement was somewhat unusual in that the cloister court lay to the south of the chancel, rather than the normal position against the nave of the priory church. This may reflect a parochial use of the nave, with the canons' liturgy centred upon the eastern end. Eventually the church passed into the hands of the Bulkeleys, a local land-owning family who built Penmon dovecot (no. 4) and the deer park.

I ST SEIRIOL'S WELL

Turn left immediately behind the wall at the far end of the car park and follow the path to the well. Notice the remains of the monastic fishpond on your right as you approach the well.

Traditionally, this well was thought to be associated with the early native Welsh monastic settlement at Penmon. Indeed, the well and adjacent 'cell', or chamber, were reputedly linked with St Seiriol himself. What survives today, however, is probably very much later. The well is one of many examples in Wales linked with a local saint. Such wells were thought to have healing powers and they continued to be visited by the sick and infirm until fairly recent times. In 1811, St Seiriol's was recorded as 'formerly in good repute'.

The well is approached from the south-east through a stone gateway. The lower courses of the stone hut or cell lie just to the left, and this is entered from the south. The well itself is situated directly ahead. In the foreground, there is now an open forecourt, with a stone bench along each side.

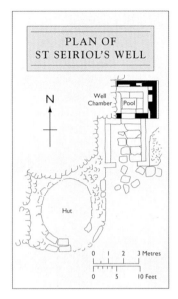

PLAN OF
ST SEIRIOL'S WELL

N

Well
Chamber · Pool

Hut

0   1   2   3 Metres

0   5   10 Feet

You will see a draw-bar hole for securing a door in the left-hand jamb of the entrance. The rectangular main chamber is situated beyond.

The well chamber is built against a vertical rock face, which forms one side of the structure. Inside, there is a small pool surrounded by a slabbed floor. It also has stone benches, wall recesses, and a probable 'squint', or viewing hole, in the right-hand corner. The upper part of the chamber has been rebuilt in brick and internally the walls retain a thick rendering of plaster. These changes seem to have taken place in the eighteenth century, whereas the lower courses are likely to be of earlier origin.

Return to the car park and climb the steps to the church. At the top, you are standing in what was the cloister of the Augustinian priory. Ahead, adjoining the south transept of the church, is the much altered dwelling, which possibly served as the prior's house. To the right is the thirteenth-century chancel of the priory church, with the earlier twelfth-century nave beyond. The church is not in the care of Cadw, but Penmon Cross is now situated within the nave. To the left are the remains of the monastic buildings, which formed the south range of the cloister.

2 PENMON CROSS

The cross is located in the nave, to the left of the entrance to the church. It originally stood in Penmon deer park, but in 1977 it was moved inside for protection.

The rectangular base, shaft, and circular head of this elaborately-carved cross are all separate stones, mortised together. The decoration on the shaft consists mainly of fret-patterns and plaits, set in panels divided by mouldings.

Such interlacing pattern was common in the tenth century and embodies Irish and Scandinavian influences, though the cross is thought to belong to a small surviving group carved by a school of craftsmen centred on Cheshire. Although much worn and difficult to see, the main scene on the front of the shaft is thought to represent the temptation of St Anthony, showing the saint facing front, flanked on either side by animal-headed demons. There is a further figure scene at the base of the left side of the shaft, comprising a small human figure and four animals.

A second cross can be seen in the south transept of the church. Its head and shaft are a single stone, and it is probably of the same period and school as the main Penmon example, though its base is a modern addition.

Above left: *Penmon Cross used to stand in the nearby deer park. In 1977 it was placed in the nave of the church for protection. The base, head, and shaft of the cross are all separate stones mortised together.*
Above right: *The decoration on the back of the Penmon Cross shows distinct Scandinavian influence (Archaeologia Cambrensis, 1919).*

The decoration on the shaft, with key patterns and knots set in panels, is similar to that on the font (located at the western end of the nave), which could have been the original base of the cross.

The south doorway in the nave of the church at Penmon. The decoration in the tympanum above the door includes a beast biting its own tail.

On leaving the church, you may wish to view the tympanum above the south nave doorway at the west end of the churchyard. It is carved with an interlaced design around a beast which is biting its own tail.

Return towards the car park and the former southern range of the monastic buildings.

3 PENMON MONASTIC BUILDINGS

At about the time the ancient church was converted to a priory of Augustinian canons, a three-storey range was built to the south of the chancel. This rectangular building, with a deeply-battered base and high gables, housed the canons' dining hall and dormitory. In the sixteenth century, a two-storey block

was added at the east end of the earlier range.

Begin your tour in the thirteenth-century range, entering through the plain, square-headed doorway into what must have served as a cellar. The regular row of beam holes in each of the side walls marks the floor of the canons' dining hall above. This was entered from an external stair (since destroyed), through the now-blocked doorway in the southern wall. Opposite, a second blocked doorway, with a pointed arch, led into the cloister. The dining hall was well lit with windows on the south side. A ledge and further beam holes over these windows indicate the position of the third storey, which is likely to have been the dormitory. There is a tall lancet window, with a moulded hood, in the west gable.

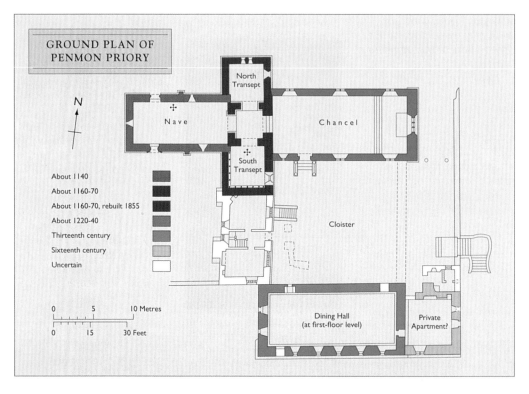

GROUND PLAN OF
PENMON PRIORY

N

About 1140
About 1160-70
About 1160-70, rebuilt 1855
About 1220-40
Thirteenth century
Sixteenth century
Uncertain

North Transept

Nave

Chancel

South Transept

Cloister

0   5   10 Metres
0   15   30 Feet

Dining Hall
(at first-floor level)

Private Apartment?

The south range of monastic buildings at Penmon. This tall gabled block had cellarage on the ground floor, with the canons' dining room above, and their dormitory on the top storey.

A plain, twelfth-century incised cross-slab can be seen against the west wall of the cellar. This was earlier used as the lintel above the entrance at this level.

Outside, you will see the very clear straight joint that marks the later addition of an almost square block at the eastern end of the dining hall and dormitory. This later building was still roofed when the Buck brothers published their engraving of Penmon in 1742 (see p. 23).

Within, at ground-floor level, there is a fireplace, which provided heat in what is sometimes interpreted as the 'warming house'. Normally, this was the only room in a monastery, apart from the infirmary, where a fire was kept burning. But such an arrangement in the sixteenth century seems unlikely, and it may well be that the room was used as a private apartment for one of the senior canons. This view is supported by the provision of a private latrine in the north-east corner.

The upper floor is also somewhat curious in terms of monastic planning. It has been suggested that it served as a kitchen, with its own fireplace. A doorway in the west wall linked this room directly to the dining hall, and another blocked entrance may have led to a further latrine. The window in the eastern gable lit an attic above.

As you leave the monastic buildings, you will see the domed roof of the dovecot at the far end of the car park.

4 PENMON DOVECOT

The dovecot was built around 1600, possibly by Sir Richard Bulkeley, whose house Baron Hill, just west of Beaumaris, was finished in 1618.

The building is square in plan and has a massive vaulted dome roof. This is crowned with an open cupola, through which the birds could fly in and out. The stone pillar inside is some 12 feet (3.7m) high and has corbelled steps. This pillar would have supported a revolving ladder, so that eggs could be collected from the numerous nests which line the walls.

The dovecot at Penmon was probably built by Sir Richard Bulkeley around 1600. The pigeons or doves housed in about 1,000 nesting boxes would have been an important source of fresh meat during the winter months.

The vaulted dome of the Penmon dovecot. Birds were allowed to fly in and out through the open cupola at the top.

Before improvements in feeding stuffs simplified the problem of fattening livestock through the winter months, the pigeons or doves housed in the 1,000 or so nests would have been considered an important source of fresh meat.

From Penmon, it is necessary to return to Beaumaris, and from the centre of the town you should turn right and take the B5109 to Pentraeth where it joins the A5025. Turn right towards Amlwch, and continue north to Llanallgo. At the roundabout, follow the minor road to Lligwy Bay, signposted to Din Lligwy. The entrance to the next monument is located a few hundred yards on the left.

5 LLIGWY BURIAL CHAMBER

(NGR SH501860)

Approaching the tomb, the original entrance can be seen on the eastern side. The chamber consists of eight low uprights supporting a massive capstone, some 18 feet long and 15 feet wide (5.5m by 4.6m). This great capstone is about 5 feet (1.5m) above the bottom of a natural fissure in the limestone rock, and the supporting uprights sit on the rock at the edge of the fissure or on rough stone walling.

The way the capstone, which weighs some 25 tons, sits so low over a pit gives the tomb a very unusual, squat appearance.

Excavations at this tomb in 1908 revealed the bones of between 15 and 30 individuals — men, women and children. Animal bones and shells were also found, together with flint implements, a bone pin and pottery. The form and decoration of the pottery indicate that the chamber was in use during the Neolithic and early Bronze Age periods.

Follow the same road about 400 yards (366m) to the north, where you will find the next monuments signposted on the left.

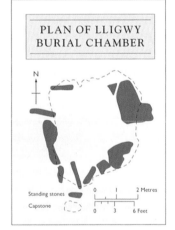

PLAN OF LLIGWY BURIAL CHAMBER

N

Standing stones

Capstone

0 1 2 Metres

0 3 6 Feet

Above left: Flint implements, pottery and a bone pin found during the 1908 excavations at Lligwy burial chamber (National Museum of Wales).
Above right: Lligwy burial chamber has a low, squat appearance, dominated by its massive capstone, which is estimated to weigh some 25 tons.

Hen Capel Lligwy lies isolated in a field within the large parish of Penrhos Lligwy. The chapel probably dates from the first half of the twelfth century and may have been intended to serve the needs of an increasing population, though it never appears to have achieved parochial status.

6 HEN CAPEL LLIGWY

(NGR SH499864)

Park at the lay-by and approach the chapel by the indicated path.

The origins of this small chapel are obscure, though its construction in stone dates from the first half of the twelfth century. It lay within the large parish of Penrhos Lligwy but, despite an expanding medieval population, never appears to have achieved parochial status itself, and remained a chapel of ease. By the early 1100s, Anglesey was finally free from Viking raids, and the Normans had abandoned their effort to hold the island. It was at this time, under the patronage of Gruffudd ap Cynan (d. 1137)

and his successor Owain Gwynedd (d. 1170), that many churches were built in masonry for the first time (p. 19). Here, at Hen Capel Lligwy, the lower parts of the walls belong to this period, though the upper parts were rebuilt in the fourteenth century. The difference in building techniques can be recognized, although the whole building is of rough coursed rubble blocks, with nothing in the way of surviving architectural detail.

As you approach, you will see that the walls survive to gable height, although the chapel is now roofless. On top of the western gable there is a small, fourteenth-century bellcote. The chapel is a simple rectangular structure, with no architectural division

between nave and chancel. It is entered from the south through a doorway with a plain, round supporting arch. Traces of render still cover areas of the internal walls, and the former east window is now blocked. The large stone lying in the nave may be the base of a churchyard cross.

The smaller chapel to the south is clearly later and was added in the sixteenth century. There was a window in each of the three external walls; the southern example is now blocked. A flight of rough stone steps leads down beneath the chapel to a small vault.

Rejoin the footpath and continue westwards as indicated across the fields to Din Lligwy.

Dry-stone walls at the late Roman native settlement of Din Lligwy. One of the two round huts in the enclosure can be seen in the centre of this view.

7 DIN LLIGWY HUT GROUP

(NGR SH496862)

Excavation in the early twentieth century recovered coins and pottery, mainly of the third and fourth centuries A.D., showing that the enclosed settlement had been occupied during the later Roman period. However, such artefacts were scarce before the arrival of the Romans so their absence does not preclude an earlier origin. Moreover, several similar settlements have been shown to have Iron Age origins, and traces of earlier structures outside the enclosure may indicate a similar development at Din Lligwy.

The site extends over about half an acre (0.2 ha), and is enclosed by a wall, 5 feet (1.5m) thick and up to 4 feet (1.2m) high, built of two rows of large limestone slabs with rubble infill. The stone was probably quarried locally. The settlement is now entered through a modern break in the enclosure wall, which leads into a rectangular building, but the original entrance lay on the south side. Several more rectangular structures are ranged along the inside of the enclosure wall, all with entrances opening towards the interior of the settlement. There is an additional rectangular building against the outside of the enclosure wall to the south.

The walls of these structures average some 3 to 5 feet (0.9m–1.5m) in height.

Two circular buildings can be seen within the enclosure: one in the north-west and the other in the south-east. That in the north-west corner is better preserved, being about 21 feet (6.4m) in diameter with walls some 7 feet (2.1m) thick. Its wide, eastern doorway has two doorsteps, while inside a small niche existed against the western wall. Excavations within the interior revealed Roman coins of the third to fourth centuries, pottery, glass and a small silver ingot.

The enclosure cannot really be considered defensive in character, and the settlement probably belonged to a farming community. It has been suggested that the round structures were houses, while the rectangular ones were barns or workshops. Certainly, the smelting hearths and iron slag found in some of these buildings during excavations suggest they had been used for metalworking.

Return along the minor road to Llanallgo where the A5025 may be rejoined. This leads directly southwards, back to Menai Bridge.

TOUR 2
WESTERN ANGLESEY

A selection of the flints and a stone bead found during the excavations at Bryn Celli Ddu (National Museum of Wales).

From the A55 at Britannia Bridge, take the A4080. Turn left for Newborough, and continue westwards for about 2½ miles (4.1km). Bryn Celli Ddu is signposted at the right turn to Llanddaniel Fab. A car park is located about 800 yards (734m) on the left.

On route you will pass Plas Newydd (new palace or mansion), a site in the care of the National Trust. The history of this site goes back some 500 years, but the present house dates from the late eighteenth century. There is much to see in the fine gardens and woodland in both summer and winter.

8 BRYN CELLI DDU BURIAL CHAMBER

(NGR SH508702)

Park in the car park and follow the signs and footpath beside the bridge on the opposite side of the road for some 700 yards (640m). A torch will be useful at this site.

Bryn Celli Ddu — the Mound in the Dark Grove — is probably the best-known prehistoric monument on the island, and is one of the most evocative archaeological sites in Britain. First explored seriously in 1865, the tomb was thoroughly excavated in 1928–29. The excavations revealed something of the long and complex history of the site.

The monument seems to have begun in the later Neolithic as a 'henge', or ritual enclosure (see pp. 6–7). It consisted of a bank (now lost) around an inner ditch, which enclosed a circle of upright stones. The ditch originally measured 69 feet (21m) in diameter, and was 17 feet (5.2m) wide and 6 feet (1.8m) deep. Its outer edge can still be seen and several stones from the inner stone circle also survive.

At a later date, towards the end of the Neolithic, the henge made way for a passage grave, a type of burial monument

found around the Irish seaboard and as far afield as Brittany. A new stone burial chamber was constructed within the henge and was covered by a substantial mound that extended into the ditch, obscuring the earlier stone circle. This mound must have been an impressive feature standing several feet in height and with a kerb of large stones around its base. The present mound is only a partial reconstruction, but the original kerb can be seen within the henge ditch and this gives an impression of the former scale of the monument.

Following the kerb around to the east, you will see that it turns inwards to join the dry-stone walling of the entrance passage leading into the burial chamber itself. The entrance was probably an important focal point for ceremonial activity. Hearths and a platform of white quartz pebbles were found in this area. When the use of the tomb finally came to an end, the outer passage and entrance were concealed with blocking. Beyond the blocking, and outside the ditch, the excavations recovered evidence of a small ox burial, found in

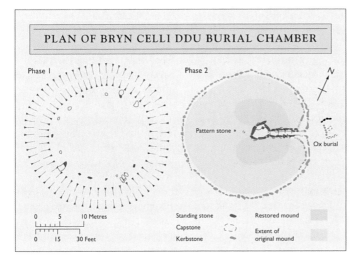

PLAN OF BRYN CELLI DDU BURIAL CHAMBER

Phase 1   Phase 2   N

Pattern stone

Ox burial

0   5   10 Metres
0   15   30 Feet

Standing stone   Restored mound
Capstone   Extent of original mound
Kerbstone

The entrance and part restored mound of Bryn Celli Ddu. The site appears to have begun as a henge monument, which was later partly incorporated into a passage grave. The kerb of stones retaining the mound was built in the partially filled ditch of the henge.

an enclosure framed with stone and timber, and now marked by small stones set in front of the tomb. Such a burial is unusual, though it is generally seen as an extension of the ritual activity in the entrance area to the tomb

The burial chamber itself is entered from the north-east by a narrow passage, 27 feet (8.2m) long and 3 feet (0.9m) wide. The passage is divided by two tall portal stones into an outer stretch, 10 feet (3m) long, which was probably never roofed, and an inner section, 16 feet (4.9m) long and 5 feet (1.5m) high. The outer passage was blocked when the tomb ceased to be used. A low shelf can be seen along the north wall of the inner passage.

The passage leads to a polygonal stone chamber, 8 feet (2.4m) wide, roofed by two capstones. As noted, the whole chamber would originally have been covered by the mound, but in the reconstruction the west side has been left open. Inside the chamber, you will see a neatly dressed free-standing pillar, almost circular in shape. One of the stones on the south wall of the chamber has a spiral design carved on it. The symbolic meaning of these features remains uncertain and the authenticity of the spiral has been questioned.

Human bones, both burnt and unburnt, were found in the chamber and passage of the tomb. Other finds were few, but included two flint arrowheads, a stone bead, and limpet and mussel shells. The absence of pottery makes it difficult to date the tomb closely.

Leaving the passage, and walking around the outside of the tomb to the back of the

chamber, there are other features of particular note. The excavations uncovered a pit, which had been dug at the centre of the henge, in which a fire had been lit and a human ear-bone placed at the bottom. Following this curious ceremony, a flat stone was placed over the pit. Nearby, another stone was discovered, larger and decorated with a meandering pattern. A cast of this has been set up to indicate its presumed original position. Both features may have played some part in the ceremonies before the henge was replaced by the passage grave, when they would have been buried by the earthen mound.

The curvilinear style of decoration on the upright stone, with wavy and spiral lines, has parallels on tombs elsewhere, especially in Brittany. The original stone is now on display at the National Museum & Gallery, in Cardiff.

The inner passage of the tomb at Bryn Celli Ddu with the central chamber beyond. Notice the shelf along the north (right) side of the passage.

Rejoin the A4080 and continue westwards, passing through Brynsiencyn. About 1 mile (1.6km) further on, look out for the entrance to the next site which is located in a lay-by on the right-hand side of the road.

The decorated 'Pattern Stone', which was discovered near a ceremonial pit at the back of the chamber at Bryn Celli Ddu. A replica of the stone has been set up at the site and the original is now in the National Museum & Gallery, Cardiff.

The large circular enclosure of Castell Bryn Gwyn (Crown copyright: Royal Commission on the Ancient and Historical Monuments of Wales).

9 CASTELL BRYN GWYN

(NGR SH464671)

Park at the lay-by and follow the trackway on foot, a distance of some 500 yards (457m).

This monument consists of a single bank, partly destroyed by farm buildings on the north side, and breached in several places in recent times. However, excavations in 1959–60 revealed a site of considerable interest, with a particularly

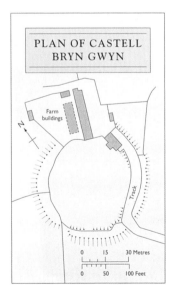

PLAN OF CASTELL BRYN GWYN

long history spanning the Neolithic to Roman periods.

The earliest phase consisted of a circular enclosure, 130 feet (39.6m) in diameter, of late Neolithic or early Bronze Age date, defined by a bank with an external ditch. Both the bank and the ditch were broken by a very narrow causeway on the south-west side. It was thought to have been a henge monument, but these generally have a ditch inside the bank. Moreover, the excavations uncovered postholes and a scatter of occupation debris within the enclosure, suggesting that it was probably a settlement surrounded by a stone rampart and flat-bottomed ditch, rather than a ritual site. Finds included flints and pottery of late Neolithic date, together with a bronze awl used for piercing leather.

There were several later additions to the bank and ditch, culminating in a timber-revetted rampart with a 'V'-shaped ditch on the line of the visible bank. Although this later use of the site cannot be well dated, the form of the enclosure was common in the Iron Age. In addition, the excavation recovered a few sherds of Roman pottery of first-century date (Flavian), indicating occupation at about this time.

Return eastwards, back along the A4080, and turn left on to the minor road, which leads towards Llangaffo (immediately before the sign for Brynsiencyn village). The entrance to the next monument is located a short distance down this road on the left. Waterproof boots are advisable at this site.

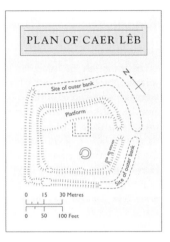

PLAN OF CAER LÊB

10 CAER LÊB

(NGR SH473674)

This rectilinear enclosure, some 200 feet (61m) long and 160 feet (48.8m) wide, is defined by double banks and ditches, with its original entrance probably near the south-eastern side. It is badly eroded in parts, the outer bank being totally destroyed on the north and east sides. Because of its low-lying and marshy location, the monument has sometimes

The rectilinear enclosure of Caer Lêb is clearly defined by its double banks and ditches (Crown copyright: Royal Commission on the Ancient and Historical Monuments of Wales).

been interpreted as a medieval moated homestead, but it is doubtful that this was its original purpose. Finds recovered during the nineteenth-century excavations included Roman pottery, a third-century brooch and a coin (denarius) of Postumus (260–69) indicating use of the site in the later Roman period. However, excavations at a very similar enclosure at Bryn Eryr, Llansadwrn, have indicated a second-century B.C. construction date; therefore, an Iron Age origin for Caer Lêb now seems more likely.

The early excavations at Caer Lêb also uncovered some internal stone buildings, including a rectangular structure near the entrance and, near the centre, a circular hut which was paved with stone slabs and contained a hearth. Other finds included quernstones and a glass stud.

Although it is possible that the settlement had its origins in later prehistory, the site clearly saw some later use, since the platform visible along the north-east side of the enclosure yielded a medieval coin.

Continue northwards along the same road, turning left then right at the crossroads, for about 1 mile (1.6km). The next monument is situated on the right.

Bodowyr burial chamber, with its large mushroom-shaped capstone.

11 BODOWYR BURIAL CHAMBER

(NGR SH462683)

This small polygonal chamber has never been excavated, but its form is characteristic of the Neolithic period. It is clearly defined by five upright stones, one of which has now fallen. In fact, only three of these now support the massive mushroom-shaped capstone, some 8 feet (2.4m) long and 6 feet (1.8m) broad. The low upright on the east side of the chamber may mark the position of the original entrance passage.

Return to the A4080 and continue westwards through Newborough. Just beyond Malltraeth, take the B4422 to Bethel. Turn left in the village, on to the minor road towards Soar, which takes a right turn on route. At Soar, turn right for Mona, and watch for the entrance to the next site about ¹/2 mile (1km) further on.

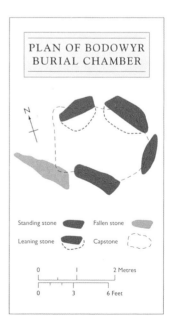

PLAN OF BODOWYR BURIAL CHAMBER

Standing stone	Fallen stone
Leaning stone	Capstone

0		1		2 Metres

0	3	6 Feet

Din Dryfol burial chamber is located on a narrow ridge which may have determined, or been chosen to accommodate, the elongated shape of the tomb. Excavations have revealed several phases of use with up to four burial chambers.

12 DIN DRYFOL BURIAL CHAMBER

(NGR SH395725)

Park at Fferam Rhosydd and follow the indicated path through the farmyard. Cross the fields on foot, a total distance of some 400 yards (370m).

Walking towards the monument you will note its position on a narrow, rocky ledge at the foot of a steep hill. The elongated shape of the tomb was perhaps determined by its location or even influenced its choice. Excavations in 1969–70 revealed several structural phases, with up to four rectangular burial chambers in all. As such, the tomb can be compared with Trefignath (pp. 46–8), and belongs to much the same period.

Approaching the tomb from the eastern edge of the ridge, the most prominent surviving feature is the tall portal stone standing in the foreground. This belonged to the latest chamber in the sequence. Beyond, you will recognize several uprights of the earliest and most westerly chamber. The capstone of this western chamber, which is some 10 feet (3m) long and 5 feet (1.5m) broad, is known to have slipped from its supports even before 1871. There are no upstanding traces of the three other chambers, one of which had included a wooden portal — a very unusual feature in these stone tombs. It seems likely that all four chambers were incorporated into a long cairn extending for up to 200 feet (62m) along the length of the ridge.

It has been suggested, from the pottery and other meagre finds, that the tomb was not used for long. It was probably built and modified in the earlier Neolithic period.

Return to Soar and turn right on to the minor road which leads north-westwards. You will pass over a crossroads, after which you must turn left, and at Pencarnisiog you pass over another crossroads before rejoining the A4080. Turn left, and look out for the 'Wayside Stores' in Llanfaelog, where (on payment of a deposit) a key can be collected for Barclodiad y Gawres. Continue along the A4080 towards Aberffraw. Alternatively, a key can be borrowed from the Coastal Heritage Project Centre, Aberffraw.

13 BARCLODIAD Y GAWRES BURIAL CHAMBER

(NGR SH328708)

You may care to use the large car park, close to the monument at Cable (Trecastell) Bay. The tomb lies some 500 yards (550m) along the cliff path. A torch is necessary, and the key can be collected at the 'Wayside Stores', Llanfaelog or the Coastal Heritage Project Centre, Aberffraw (see above).

The spectacular cliffside position of this later Neolithic monument is one of its great attractions, and provides a short pleasant walk. The name means 'the Giantess's Apronful' and is derived from local tradition. The tomb was thought to hold little of value until the excavations of 1952–53 revealed a series of striking discoveries.

The mound seen today is a reconstruction, though it is based on the original Neolithic form. The tomb builders raised a largely earthen mound some 90 feet (27m) in diameter. Parts of this tumulus were made up of peat turfs, and the edge was loosely defined by a tight packing of stones.

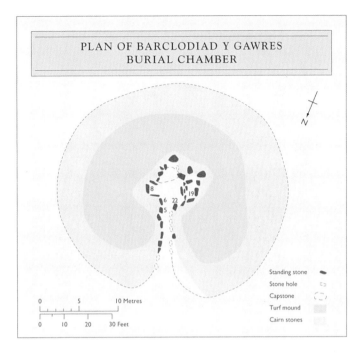

PLAN OF BARCLODIAD Y GAWRES BURIAL CHAMBER

Standing stone
Stone hole
Capstone
Turf mound
Cairn stones

An aerial view of Barclodiad y Gawres showing its spectacular coastal location overlooking Cable (Trecastell) Bay (Cambridge University Collection, copyright reserved, AOG–2).

An imaginative reconstruction of a ritual scene within the central area of the tomb at Barclodiad y Gawres, around 3000 B.C. Excavations discovered a 'stew', which seems to have been poured over the embers of a glowing fire, perhaps as an act of some special significance (National Museum of Wales).

The tomb passage itself is entered from the north. It is some 23 feet (7m) long and is flanked by upright stones. This leads to a cross-shaped (cruciform) chamber, from which open three smaller side chambers to the east, west and south. Each of these would have been covered with a capstone, but only that to the south survives. The plan of the western chamber is the most complex; the front is blocked and it has a small annexe to the south. In this, the cremated remains of two men were found, together with two burnt and broken pins of bone or antler. Traces of bone were also recovered from the east and south side chambers.

The central area of the tomb does not, however, appear to

THE DECORATED STONES

Five of the stones within the passage grave at Barclodiad y Gawres were found to have decoration. Stone 5 (see plan), though weathered, had its whole surface covered with zig-zags and lozenges. The design on Stone 6 is found on the lower right-hand side of the face, and consists of a pair of concentric circles with a lozenge below. Stone 8 is most impressive, with four spirals across the face, diminishing in size from left to right. Stone 19 is much weathered, and all that remains are traces of a small spiral, a little above mid-height and slightly right of centre. Finally, Stone 22 is the most striking of all, with a clear pattern in deep-pocked lines over the whole of the main face.

Above: Stone 22, with its striking, deeply-pocked decoration clearly visible.

Stone 8

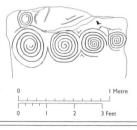

Stone 6

Stone 5

A view within the restored mound at Barclodiad y Gawres, looking from the western chamber. In the distance is Stone 8, with its spiral decoration, and to the right is the southern chamber with its capstone.

have been used for burial; instead it was used for ritual purposes. The excavations uncovered traces of a fire, which appears to have burned for some time. With the embers still glowing, a 'stew' was poured over it, and the whole quenched with a cover of limpet shells and pebbles. The 'stew' itself was hardly edible, and from the tiny bones recovered we know it contained frog, toad, snake, mouse, hare, eel, wrasse and whiting.

The excavations also uncovered one of the most exciting finds on a megalithic monument in Wales. The end stones of the east and west side chambers, and three of the inner passage stones, were found to be decorated with a variety of lightly pecked and incised designs of spirals, chevrons, zig-zags and lozenges. This type of decoration was clearly invested with some significant meaning, as it occurs elsewhere on tombs of the Neolithic period. It is particularly well known from the Irish cruciform tombs, notably in the Boyne valley.

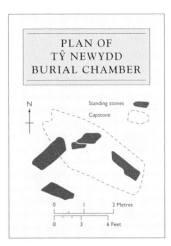

PLAN OF TŶ NEWYDD BURIAL CHAMBER

N

Standing stones

Capstone

0   1   2 Metres

0   3   6 Feet

Return the key and travel northwards on the A4080. Just beyond Llanfaelog, turn left on to the minor road to Bryngwran. The next monument is signposted, about 650 yds (600m) on the right.

14 TŶ NEWYDD BURIAL CHAMBER

(NGR SH344738)

This oval burial chamber is approached from the west. The uprights are covered by a large damaged capstone, 12 feet (3.7m) by 5 feet (1.5m), which now has additional support from two built-up pillars. A nineteenth-century account of the monument indicates that it was probably once covered by a round cairn.

The burial chamber of Tŷ Newydd. Sadly, the capstone needs the support of two built-up pillars.

The current ring of small bollards marks the protected area of the tomb.

Tŷ Newydd was excavated in 1936, but the meagre finds are not particularly useful for a close dating of the site. They included fragments of beaker pottery (p. 9) and a flint arrowhead of early Bronze Age date. The overall form of the tomb, however, suggests that initially it was constructed in the Neolithic period.

Continue north up this minor road to the A5 at Bryngwran. Turn left towards Holyhead, and in about 1 1/2 miles (2.4km) turn right at the crossroads, on to the minor road to

Bodedern, turning right again about 1/2 mile (0.8km) on. At Bodedern, turn right on to the B5109, and then left on to the minor road to Presaddfed about 1/2 mile (0.8km) on. There is a car park a short way along the road on the left. The entrance to the next monument is on the right.

15 PRESADDFED BURIAL CHAMBER

(NGR SH347808)

Walk along the small road past the estate lodge to the monument on the left side of the drive.

As you approach this monument from the south, you will see the remains of two small burial chambers, side by side, almost 7 feet (2.1m) apart. This double arrangement, with no clear access between the chambers, is reminiscent of Trefignath (pp. 46–8) and may indicate different phases of use in the Neolithic period.

The southern chamber is the better preserved, with its capstone supported on four uprights. The chamber

to the north has collapsed, although the damaged capstone and two uprights can still be seen. In the eighteenth century the tomb apparently provided shelter for a family of squatters.

Continue for about 3/4 mile (1.2km). Turn left at a 'T' junction. The entrance to Tregwehelydd Farm is about 1/2 mile (0.8km) along on the right.

16 TREGWEHELYDD STANDING STONE

(NGR SH342832)

Park in the farmyard (after asking permission from the farmer, who may help with directions), and follow the footpath, keeping close to the field edges, for a total distance of some 700 yards (650m). Approach the monument directly from the west.

Walking towards this once impressive early Bronze Age standing stone, you will appreciate its isolated but prominent position. For some distance around, it stands out from the surrounding fields, located on the crest of an east–west ridge. Sadly, the stone is now in a fragmentary state. The three sheared sections have been bolted and clamped together.

The minor road continues westwards to join the A5025. Turn left, and at Valley join the A5, and then the A55, which may be followed back to Menai Bridge. Before leaving this area, you may be interested to detour northwards to visit Llynon Mill at Llandeusant (SH 340852). This is a typical and complete example of an Anglesey tower windmill.

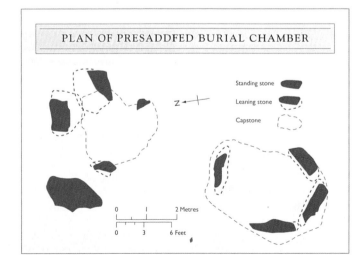

PLAN OF PRESADDFED BURIAL CHAMBER

Standing stone
Leaning stone
Capstone

z

0   1   2 Metres

0   3   6 Feet

Presaddfed burial chamber consists of two small chambers side by side and is reminiscent of the complex multi-period tomb at Trefignath (pp. 46–8).

TOUR 3
HOLYHEAD

The northern wall at Caer Gybi. The herringbone pattern of masonry, in the foreground, is quite typical of late Roman fortifications.

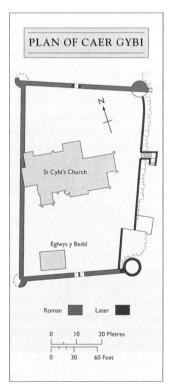

PLAN OF CAER GYBI

St Cybi's Church

Eglwys y Bedd

Roman   Later

0   10   20 Metres

0   30   60 Feet

17 CAER GYBI ROMAN FORT

(NGR SH247826)

Take the A5, or A55, into the town centre of Holyhead, and park in one of the central car parks. The Roman fort and St Cybi's church are well signposted.

The position of this site on a low sea-side cliff, together with the suggestion of an enclosed quay, have given rise to its interpretation as a late Roman coastal fort. Although there is no direct dating evidence from the site, indications from excavations on Roman forts elsewhere in Wales — notably at Cardiff, Loughor and Neath — have demonstrated a system of late Roman coastal defence. Caer Gybi may well have been

part of such a consolidated network, defending the Welsh coast from Irish raiders. It may have been linked with the late Roman watchtower and signal station on Caer y Tŵr (p. 45), and a possible second example on Carmel Head.

Caer Gybi is a sub-rectangular fort, about 246 feet (75m) by 148 feet (45m) in size. Its mortared rubble walls, standing up to 13 feet (4m) high and 5 feet (1.5m) thick, are extremely well preserved. To get the best impression of the original walls, look at the outside of the west wall and the adjacent north-west tower. There were originally four corner towers, though that in the south-west is mostly destroyed or masked by modern buildings. That in the north-east corner, overlooking the harbour, stands to a height of 26 feet (7.9m), although the top is a medieval or modern rebuild.

The northern archway, through which you may have entered the fort, is modern, not original. Inside, on the right and to the rear of this entrance, the wall is very well preserved. To the left, on the seaward side, you will get an appreciation of the high platform on which the fort was built, overlooking the dock. In this area, the curtain wall projects slightly beyond the north-east tower. This has led to the suggestion that there was originally a quay on this side of the fort. Continuing south through the interior of the fort, further details of the walls can be seen ahead and to the left. The double archway in the south wall may mark the position of a gate.

The fort is traditionally the site of a Christian monastic

foundation granted to
St Cybi by King Maelgwn
of Gwynedd in the sixth
century. The later medieval
church (thirteenth century;
extensively rebuilt in the late
fifteenth and early sixteenth
centuries), which now stands
within the walls, may be on
the site of this foundation.
The smaller chapel in the
south-west corner of the
enclosure is known as
Eglwys y Bedd (Church of
the Grave). Such churches
are traditionally believed
to cover the grave of the
founding saint.

From the centre of Holyhead
you should take the minor road
westwards to South Stack.

18 HOLYHEAD MOUNTAIN HUT GROUP

(NGR SH212820)

There is a car park on the left a
short way before South Stack, where
the lighthouse dates to the early
nineteenth century. The car park is
owned by the RSPB and marks the
beginning of a 'nature trail'.

This unenclosed settlement
lies along the foot of Holyhead
Mountain, and is often
referred to as the Tŷ Mawr
hut group. About twenty
structures remain, though
originally the group was much
larger. Over fifty buildings
were recorded in the 1860s,

and were spread over an
area of around 15 to 20 acres
(6–8.1 ha). The main surviving
group lies to the west, as you
first approach the monument,
but there is another smaller
group further east.

Pioneering excavations
were undertaken in the
mid-nineteenth century by
William Owen Stanley.
His work recovered artefacts
of Roman date, including
coins, pottery, and traces of
metalworking, and gradually
the Holyhead huts came to be
regarded as a classic Romano-
British village. However,
excavations undertaken in
the eastern group between
1978 and 1982, supported
by radiocarbon dates, have
revealed a much fuller and
more intriguing settlement
history at Tŷ Mawr.

The picture which has
emerged suggests a group
of perhaps eight distinct
farmsteads or homesteads,
only one or two of which
may have been occupied at
any one time. The evidence
for settlement certainly goes
back into the last 500 years
B.C., and extends through
to the post-Roman centuries.
As time passed, the focus
of activity in the settlement
drifted from one end to
the other, and perhaps back
again. Moreover, occupation
along the footslopes of
Holyhead Mountain goes
back even further, to the
late Neolithic or early Bronze
Age. Indeed, excavations
have revealed a collection
of even earlier Mesolithic
flint tools (p. 4).

Entering the site today,
you will see a circular building
immediately to the left.
This stone-built structure,

The port and town of Holyhead from the top of nearby Holyhead Mountain.
The Roman fort of Caer Gybi lies in the centre of the modern town and has
been interpreted as a late Roman coastal fort, which may have been linked
with the watchtower and signal station here on Caer y Twr (p. 45).

26 feet (7.9m) in diameter, was entered from the south-east. It is defined by dry-stone walling and boulders set upright. There is a raised shelf on the northern side.

Following a path around the monument, similar circular houses can be traced — some with elaborate entrances and others with internal stone furniture in the form of

benches and basins. Among these buildings or huts are a number of sunken chambers, reminiscent of Scottish souterrains, which may have been used as storage structures.

Follow the footpath eastwards to see the second smaller hut group. Nearby, another path leads towards the summit of Holyhead Mountain. This is quite a lengthy and difficult walk which only those who are reasonably fit and have strong footwear should attempt. You should allow around one to two hours for the walk.

One of the circular huts in the unenclosed settlement at the foot of Holyhead Mountain.

An imaginative reconstruction of one of the homesteads on Holyhead Mountain. The drawing shows the farmstead as it may have looked in its final phase, sometime in the late first millennium B.C. (Illustration by Jean Williamson).

19 CAER Y TŴR HILLFORT

(NGR SH218830)

Keep to the footpath which skirts the west side of the summit, entering the monument from the northern side.

Although difficult to date closely, Caer y Tŵr is very similar in form to other Iron Age hillforts in north Wales. Its superb location, crowning the summit of Holyhead Mountain, matches other such monuments in the region. There are glorious views in all directions from the hillfort, including down to Holyhead harbour and across to the rolling landscape of the island proper.

Following the path on the west side of the fort, you will see the line of the rampart against the skyline. It is difficult to pick out at first amid the rocky crags of the mountain, but it becomes clearer on approaching the north side. On this north side the rampart is seen to continue eastwards.

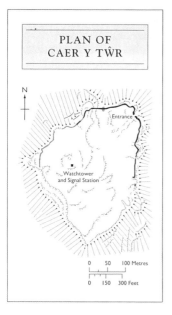

PLAN OF
CAER Y TŴR

N

Entrance

Watchtower
and Signal Station

0   50   100 Metres

0   150   300 Feet

An aerial view of the hillfort of Caer y Tŵr from the north-east. The stone rampart is clearly visible on the rocky summit of Holyhead Mountain (Cambridge University Collection: copyright reserved, AOG–25).

Entering the hillfort through the entrance in its north-east corner, notice how the rampart turns inwards to meet rocky outcrops and forms an imposing passageway. The wall can be seen clearly to the right. In places it still rises some 10 feet (3m) high and is 13 feet (4m) wide, thick enough to have accommodated a rampart walk. In total, the rampart encloses an area of about 17 acres (6.9ha), but no structures can be identified on the rocky surface of the interior with the exception of the foundations of a late Roman watchtower and signal station (see box alongside).

On leaving the car park from these monuments, turn right and follow the minor road southwards towards Trearddur Bay for about 1 mile (1.6km). At the next fork, bear left and you will see Penrhos Feilw standing stones signposted on the left-hand side.

CAER Y TŴR WATCHTOWER
AND SIGNAL STATION

The excavated Roman watchtower and signal station at the summit of Holyhead Mountain.

At the very highest point on the mountain, within Caer y Tŵr hillfort, the remains of a Roman watchtower and signal station can be seen. The structure was 20 feet (6.1m) square, and pottery and coins recovered during excavations date it to the late fourth century A.D. The watchtower undoubtedly commanded an excellent view over Holyhead harbour and beyond, and may have been linked to the Roman coastal defence at Caer Gybi (pp. 42–3).

Penrhos Feilw standing stones. Each of the two slabs of Holyhead schist stands almost 10 feet high.

20 PENRHOS FEILW STANDING STONES

(NGR SH227809)

This impressive pair of Bronze Age standing stones are situated some 11 feet (3.3m) apart, and are up to 10 feet (3m) high. There is a long but unsubstantiated tradition that they were originally at the centre of a stone circle, and that a stone cist containing bones, spearheads and arrowheads was found between them.

Return to the road fork, turning left, and then left again on to the minor road leading to the B4545. Turn south (right) at this road, which leads towards Trearddur Bay. You need to branch off left in about 500 yds (0.5 km) into Cyttir Road and then turn right almost immediately, into Ty'n Pwll Road. The next monument will be seen in the fields to the right.

21 TŶ MAWR STANDING STONE

(NGR SH254810)

Approaching this well-preserved and imposing standing stone of Bronze Age date from the east, its isolated position on a slight rise stands out clearly. It is 9 feet (2.8m) high, and tapers slightly towards the top.

Continue southwards along the same road for about 1/2 mile (0.8km). The entrance to the final monument is on the left.

Tŷ Mawr standing stone is some 9 feet (2.8m) high, and stands isolated in a field.

22 TREFIGNATH BURIAL CHAMBER

(NGR SH259805)

This monument is approached from the west and beyond it, on the far side, there is a panel providing interpretative information.

This tomb was excavated in 1977–79, and was consolidated and laid out for public display. Three structural phases can now be clearly made out, each represented by a stone burial chamber with a covering mound. Pottery and human bones were discovered when the tomb was disturbed in the eighteenth century. The excavations uncovered stone and flint implements, together with pottery of Neolithic date from beneath the tomb itself. These suggest that the site was occupied prior to the construction of the first burial chamber.

The earliest chamber (1) is that to the western end (the nearest to the

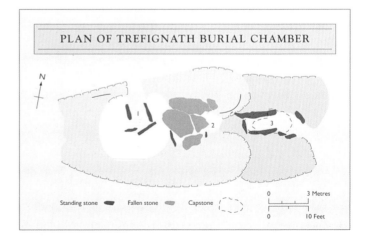

PLAN OF TREFIGNATH BURIAL CHAMBER

N

Standing stone ▬   Fallen stone ▬   Capstone

0   3 Metres

0   10 Feet

These impressive portal stones mark the entrance to the third and last chamber at Trefignath.

site entrance). It consists of a simple box-like structure, surrounded by a cairn of boulders, and may have been raised around 3750–3500 B.C. This was succeeded by the central chamber (2), which has collapsed; only one entrance stone and the back stone now stand, but a fallen side stone and the broken capstone can also be seen. Its forecourt and wedge-shaped covering mound, which incorporated the first phase chamber, was retained by a dry-stone wall.

The final, eastern, chamber (3) survives in more or less its original form. Its stone retaining wall abutted the earlier cairn material, clearly showing it to be a later addition. This chamber has two capstones supported on five uprights (aided by a modern plinth in the north-east corner). The existing mound was extended to cover this chamber, although it may never have hidden the impressively tall portal stones at the entrance. This final wedge-shaped mound had a horn-shaped recessed forecourt which is still clearly defined.

Evidence from the excavations suggests that the final closure of the chambers did not take place until perhaps after 2250 B.C. The use of a tomb over such a long period serves to emphasize the significance of such monuments in the Neolithic landscape.

The A55 may be rejoined at Holyhead.

Trefignath burial chamber was raised in three structural phases and appears to have been in use for up to 1,500 years.

FURTHER READING

Acknowledgments
The authors and Cadw would like to thank the following people for their assistance: Professor M. Aldhouse-Green, R. J. Brewer, Professor R. R. Davies, Professor W. Davies, F. M. Lynch, Dr L. Macinnes and Professor A. W. R. Whittle.

C. J. Arnold and J. L. Davies, *Roman and Early Medieval Wales* (Stroud 2000).

A. D. Carr, *Medieval Anglesey* (Llangefni 1982).

W. Davies, *Wales in the Early Middle Ages* (Leicester 1982).

F. M. Lynch, editor, *Museum of Welsh Antiquities Bangor: Catalogue of Archaeological Material* (Bangor 1986).

F. M. Lynch, *Prehistoric Anglesey*, second edition (Llangefni 1991).

F. M. Lynch, *A Guide to Ancient and Historic Wales — Gwynedd* second edition (Cardiff 2001).

F. M. Lynch, S. Aldhouse-Green and J. L. Davies, *Prehistoric Wales* (Stroud, 2000)

V. E. Nash-Williams, *The Roman Frontier in Wales*, second edition, edited by M.G. Jarrett (Cardiff 1969).

Royal Commission on Ancient and Historical Monuments in Wales and Monmouthshire, *An Inventory of the Ancient Monuments in Anglesey* (London 1937).

A. J. Taylor, *Beaumaris Castle*, revised edition (Cadw, Cardiff 1998).

J. A. Taylor, editor, *Culture and Environment in Prehistoric Wales* (Oxford 1980).